ABRSM
PUBLISHING

music medals

clarinet

options practice book

sample download pages – pupil's copy

C000161713

music medals

The Associated Board of the Royal Schools of Music

Copper Options

Pupil's Page

Royal Academy of Music
Royal College of Music
Royal Northern College of Music
Royal Scottish Academy of Music and Drama

ASSOCIATED BOARD
OF THE ROYAL SCHOOLS OF MUSIC

Make a Tune

Set 1 *or*

Set 2

Sight-Reading

Bronze Options
Pupil's Page

Make a Tune

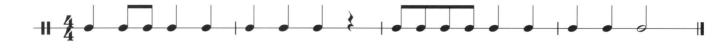

Question & Answer

Sight-Reading

Silver Options
Pupil's Page

Royal Academy of Music
Royal College of Music
Royal Northern College of Music
Royal Scottish Academy of Music and Drama

ASSOCIATED BOARD
OF THE ROYAL SCHOOLS OF MUSIC

Make a Tune (in F major)

Question & Answer

Sight-Reading

Gold Options
Pupil's Page

Royal Academy of Music
Royal College of Music
Royal Northern College of Music
Royal Scottish Academy of Music and Drama

ASSOCIATED BOARD
OF THE ROYAL SCHOOLS OF MUSIC

Make a Tune (in A minor)

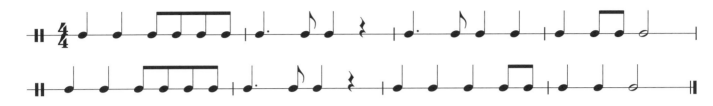

Question & Answer

Sight-Reading

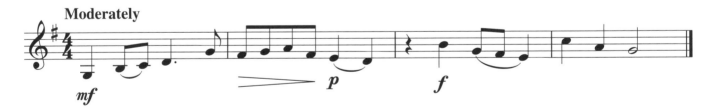

Platinum Options

Pupil's Page

Royal Academy of Music
Royal College of Music
Royal Northern College of Music
Royal Scottish Academy of Music and Drama

ASSOCIATED BOARD
OF THE ROYAL SCHOOLS OF MUSIC

Make a Tune (in B♭ major)

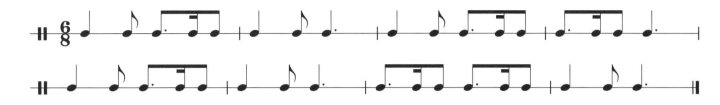

Question & Answer

Sight-Reading

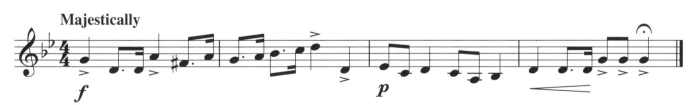

**The Associated Board of
the Royal Schools of Music
(Publishing) Limited**

24 Portland Place
London W1B 1LU
United Kingdom

www.abrsmpublishing.co.uk

Contents

See insert for pupil's pages

The Music Medals Syllabus and the Ensemble and Options materials
were devised on behalf of ABRSM by Nigel Scaife, Syllabus Principal.

© 2004 by The Associated Board of the Royal Schools of Music

No part of this publication may be copied or reproduced in any
form or by any means without the prior permission of the publisher.

Music origination by Artemis Music.
Design by Warsaw.
Photography by Guy Drayton.
Printed in England by Caligraving Ltd, Thetford, Norfolk

Introduction

Welcome to this book of practice tests for Options, the third section of Music Medals. This introduction outlines the basis of the tests and shows how they relate to typical lesson activities aimed at developing essential musicianship skills, including improvisation and sight-reading. Group teaching offers ideal opportunities for developing these skills as for many pupils these are best developed in collaboration with others.

These Options have been designed to build on and support the kind of rhythm games and 'taking turns' activities that group teachers use to develop musical understanding and awareness. They work particularly well within the context of scale practice and learning to play and think in keys. Activities that build awareness of melodic shape and direction, both by ear and at sight, and of basic harmony (for when taking the higher Medals) will develop the skills that are to be assessed.

Options help to build sound musicianship skills. While it is expected that candidates will play to their strengths in the Medal, it is hoped that teachers will encourage pupils to develop their ability in the full range of activities covered by these tests, within a general framework of creativity, game-playing and experimentation.

The Tests and Assessment

The candidate must choose one of the following four Options:

- Call & Response
- Make a Tune
- Question & Answer
- Sight-Reading

When selecting, pupils can therefore choose a test which best displays their developing skills. Those who are particularly fluent with notation may wish to choose the Sight-Reading Option, while others will prefer to use their creativity in the Make a Tune test by improvising a short melody using a given rhythm. Call & Response also nurtures improvisation skills, with the candidate reacting to a melodic stimulus given by the Teacher-Assessor. Question & Answer combines the elements of sight-reading and creativity.

On the assessment day, the Teacher-Assessor will have a set of personalized confidential tests for each candidate, downloaded from the Board's website at **www.musicmedals.org**. As well as providing practice tests for each Option, at each level, the present book contains examples of the download pages (32–6) for the purpose of mock assessments. Before seeing the set of tests, the candidate must have decided which Option he or she wishes to take (as opposed to looking at the tests and then deciding). In the case of Make a Tune,

Question & Answer and Sight-Reading, half a minute of preparation time is allowed, during which time the candidate may try out any part of the test on his or her instrument. Assessment is made only of the performance itself and not the preparation.

Each set of tests in this book is preceded by a 'rubric' – a formal set of words that the Teacher-Assessor might use to introduce the activity. However, having prepared pupils for their Options over an extended period of time, it is unlikely that Teacher-Assessors will need to quote the full rubric on the day, although they may do so if they wish. When giving the pulse and counting in, it is best to beat time/click *and* count the beats out loud. Always give two bars in.

Call & Response

Call & Response is typical of the interactive activities and rhythm games that feature in many group lessons. Through participating in a variety of these, pupils' listening skills, technical ability and knowledge of the instrument are developed, as well as their confidence and general musical awareness. A range of different challenges can be introduced over time that will help develop control and shaping of the melody. Discussion of what constitutes continuity and balance between the call and response, with reference to the Music Medals solo or ensemble pieces (or other repertoire), will enrich pupils' understanding and their fund of ideas.

This test is taken entirely by ear and is designed to develop listening and responding skills. The candidate is required to provide a musical response on his or her instrument to each of two separate short phrases of unfamiliar music played by the Teacher-Assessor. The key is stated, and the starting note of the first phrase named and played, by the Teacher-Assessor, who also counts in two bars before playing the first phrase. The musical interaction should be continuous, in time and without a break.

The first phrase is notated, while the second of the Teacher-Assessor's 'calls' is improvised, in response to the candidate's first phrase. The second call takes up the candidate's musical ideas, so that the test becomes a kind of dialogue.

Pupils should aim to give fluent responses that are well shaped and that have an imaginative connection with the calls. The range of keys for this Option, which is the same for Sight-Reading, is given below, under 'Musical Parameters'.

You will notice that parts played by the teacher sometimes carry marks of articulation, particularly slurs. This is to give the phrase a more defined musical character, providing a springboard for the pupil's response. It is not necessary in the assessment that candidates copy this articulation when responding.

Make a Tune

Making up short tunes based on a scale or smaller set of notes reinforces finger patterns, helps develop thinking in the chosen key and raises awareness of melodic shape, including the expressive effect of different intervals. In working through this book (or other suitable materials) when preparing for this test, pupils will develop a sense of the tonic, the function of the leading note and a deeper understanding of the diatonic system. The understanding of harmony can be developed further using chord shapes and symbols in conjunction with the given rhythms.

The intention is for candidates to act creatively and invent something with melodic character, rather than simply to map a scale or scalic pattern on to the given rhythm. At all levels, pupils should be encouraged to phrase their tunes expressively and to think about shape, direction and dynamics. To achieve an Excellent result, the tune must follow the given rhythm and contain an appropriate plus imaginative choice of pitches.

Copper and Bronze

The candidate is required to make up a tune on his or her instrument using a given rhythm at a set speed, following half a minute of preparation. At Copper and Bronze levels, candidates can take the test by ear or at sight (from notation). When taken by ear, the rhythm is clapped following a two-bar count-in. This is repeated a second and third time, after which the candidate is given half a minute to prepare before being asked to play his or her tune.

When taking the test at sight, candidates are given the notated rhythm, then the pulse, and half a minute of preparation time before being counted in for two bars. Because some teachers use crotchets and quavers first while others use minims and crotchets, the tests at Copper level are written in two versions, from which the Teacher-Assessor chooses.

At Copper and Bronze levels, candidates must use at least three pitches to pass.

Silver to Platinum

The candidate is required to make up a tune on his or her instrument using a given rhythm and in a specified key; the rhythm is given in notation only. After being given two bars of the pulse, candidates have half a minute of preparation time before being counted in by the Teacher-Assessor (for two bars).

To pass at Silver, Gold and Platinum, candidates must use at least five pitches.

Question & Answer

This test covers two main skills: the ability to assimilate a short phrase (by ear, at Copper level, or from notation, at Bronze and above), and then to play it back accurately and musically; and the ability to improvise a response to that phrase (Bronze to Platinum levels).

Copper

The candidate is required to repeat on his or her instrument two separate one-bar rhythms in 4/4, in time and as an echo. The Teacher-Assessor should either play the rhythms on one note or clap them. No time is given for preparation.

The answers may be played on a single note or on a series of notes, although there is no additional credit for using more than one note. The Teacher-Assessor counts in two bars before the first rhythm.

Bronze to Platinum

The candidate is required to play at sight a two-bar passage of unfamiliar music and to improvise a two-bar answering phrase. After giving two bars of the pulse, the Teacher-Assessor allows the candidate half a minute of preparation time and then gives a two-bar count-in.

Pupils should aim at creating a fluent musical phrase. This should contain all the details of the notated 'question' and continue with a well-shaped and balanced answering phrase.

Sight-Reading

The advantages of developing pupils' ability to read unfamiliar music at sight are widely acknowledged: they will be able to learn music faster, will become more musically independent, and a great deal of time is saved through not having to correct misreading of notation.

The Sight-Reading Option tests are all four bars long. There are no tempo indications as candidates are encouraged to establish an appropriate tempo for themselves, taking into account the speed at which they can play the music while maintaining a steady pulse and, at the higher levels, the character of the music.

The tests at Silver, Gold and Platinum levels carry indications of character. These are intended to help players express the content to their best ability. The choice of tempo is the player's, though a speed suiting the music's character will probably result in a more successful performance.

Teacher-Assessors will advise candidates that they may try out any part or parts of the test for half a minute before playing the whole test. To achieve an Excellent result, candidates need to play the phrase accurately and with fluency, demonstrating musical awareness. The performance should also be musically expressive, particularly at the higher Medals.

Musical Parameters

Carefully graded, the Options share certain technical and musical features at each level. These are given below, as a means of helping teachers who wish to supplement the examples in this book by creating new tests. Since not all four Options use the full range of parameters, the table must be read in conjunction with the practice tests in this book. When writing new practice tests for pupils, teachers should follow the table *and* examples.

This table shows the introduction of elements at each level. To establish the full parameters of any one medal, regard its rhythmic values, keys etc. as being **in addition** to those included earlier in the table.

Key: **CR** – Call & Response; **MT** – Make a Tune; **QA** – Question & Answer; **SR** – Sight-Reading.

copper

Pitch	
Key	C and F majors
Time signature	CR, QA, SR $\frac{4}{4}$ MT $\frac{4}{4}$ or $\frac{2}{4}$
Rhythm	

bronze

Pitch	
Key	G major
Time signature	SR $\frac{3}{4}$ MT $\frac{4}{4}$ only
Rhythm	

silver

Pitch		
Key	A minor (**MT** C and F majors)	
Time signature	CR, MT, QA $\frac{3}{4}$	
Rhythm		
Articulation and dynamics	QA SR	2-note slur 2-note slur, $\boldsymbol{f}$, $\boldsymbol{p}$
Character indication	SR	Boldly, Gently, Lilting, Lively, March, Moderately, Sadly, Smoothly

gold

Pitch		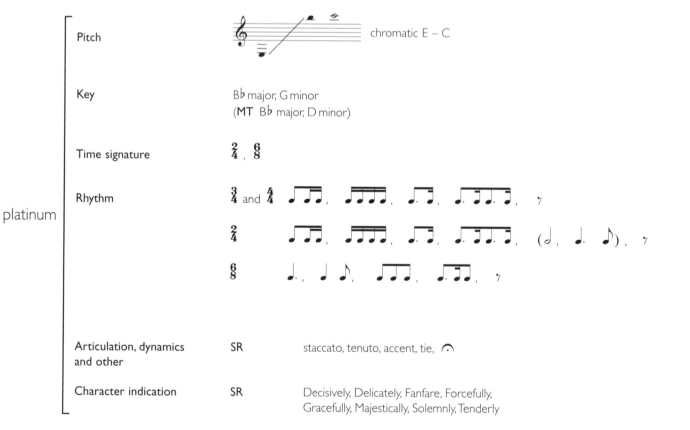 chromatic E – B
Key	D minor (**MT** G major, A minor)	
Rhythm	$\frac{4}{4}$ 𝅗𝅭 , 𝅘𝅥𝅮	
	$\frac{3}{4}$ 𝅗𝅭 , 𝅘𝅥𝅮 ♩♩♩♩♩♩	
Articulation and dynamics	QA SR	3- and 4-note slurs 3- and 4-note slurs, *mf* , *mp* , ⟨ , ⟩
Character indication	SR	Brightly, Briskly, Broadly, Calmly, Lullaby, Stately, Sweetly, Waltz

platinum

Pitch		chromatic E – C
Key	B♭ major, G minor (**MT** B♭ major, D minor)	
Time signature	$\frac{2}{4}$, $\frac{6}{8}$	
Rhythm	$\frac{3}{4}$ and $\frac{4}{4}$ ♫♫, ♬♬, ♩♩, ♩♩♩, 𝄾	
	$\frac{2}{4}$ ♫♫, ♬♬, ♩♩, ♩♩♩, (𝅗𝅥 , 𝅗𝅭 𝅘𝅥𝅮) , 𝄾	
	$\frac{6}{8}$ 𝅗𝅭 , 𝅘𝅥 𝅘𝅥𝅮 , ♫♫ , ♩♫ , 𝄾	
Articulation, dynamics and other	SR	staccato, tenuto, accent, tie, ⌢
Character indication	SR	Decisively, Delicately, Fanfare, Forcefully, Gracefully, Majestically, Solemnly, Tenderly

8

copper

Call & Response

I'm going to play you a phrase and then I want you to answer me. I'll then continue with another phrase for you to answer.
We're in … (key) and my first note is … (pitch, named and played). I'll count myself in for two bars.

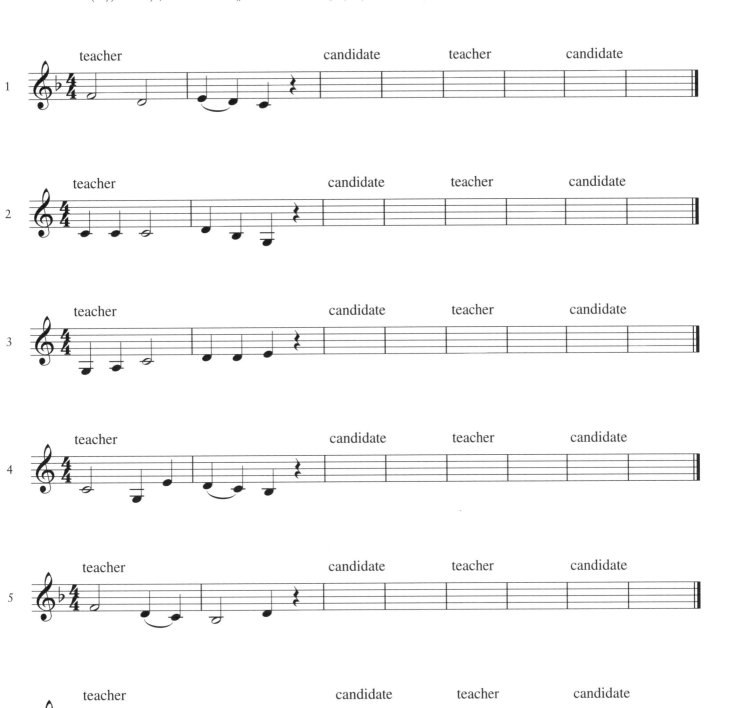

Make a Tune

By ear *You're going to make a tune using at least three pitches. Use the rhythm that I'm about to clap; you'll hear this three times. You'll then have half a minute to prepare. This is the pulse (two bars at ♩ = c.108). Here's the rhythm for the first/second/third time. After half a minute: I'll now count you in for two bars (at ♩ = c.108).*

At sight *You're going to make a tune using this rhythm and at least three pitches. This is the pulse (two bars at ♩ = c.108). You now have half a minute to try it out. After half a minute: I'll now count you in for two bars (at ♩ = c.108).*

Set 1

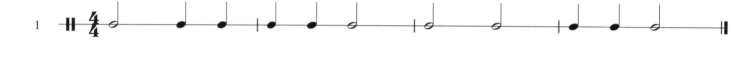

Make a Tune

By ear *You're going to make a tune using at least three pitches. Use the rhythm that I'm about to clap; you'll hear this three times. You'll then have half a minute to prepare. This is the pulse (two bars at ♩ = c.54). Here's the rhythm for the first/second/third time. After half a minute: I'll now count you in for two bars (at ♩ = c.54).*

At sight *You're going to make a tune using this rhythm and at least three pitches. This is the pulse (two bars at ♩ = c.54). You now have half a minute to try it out. After half a minute: I'll now count you in for two bars (at ♩ = c.54).*

Set 2

Question & Answer

You will hear two rhythms in 4 time (at ♩ = c.108). After each rhythm, play it back in time and as an echo. You can use just one pitch, or more if you wish. I'll count in two bars (at ♩ = c.108) before giving the first rhythm.

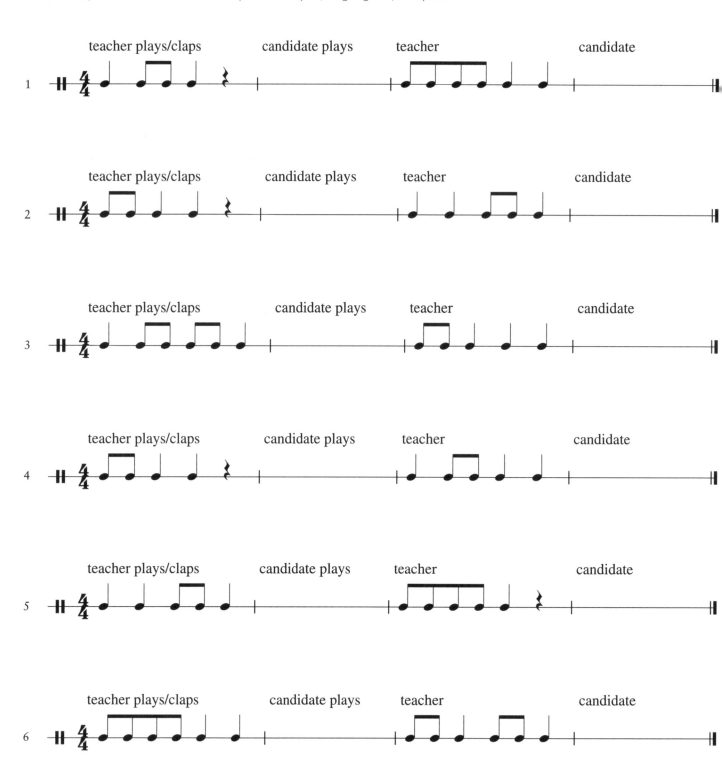

AB 3031

Sight-Reading

You have half a minute to look through this piece of music and, if you wish, try out any part or parts of it on your instrument.
I'll then ask you to play it.

bronze

Call & Response

I'm going to play you a phrase and then I want you to answer me. I'll then continue with another phrase for you to answer.
We're in … (key) and my first note is … (pitch, named and played). I'll count myself in for two bars.

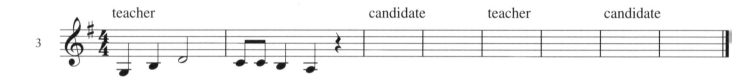

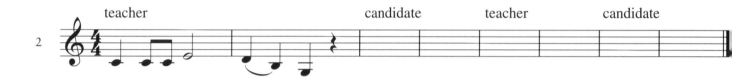

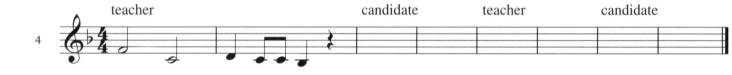

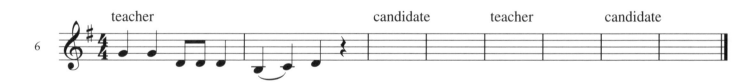

AB 3031

Make a Tune

By ear *You're going to make a tune using at least three pitches. Use the rhythm that I'm about to clap; you'll hear this three times. You'll then have half a minute to prepare. This is the pulse (two bars at ♩ = c.108). Here's the rhythm for the first/second/third time. After half a minute: I'll now count you in for two bars (at ♩ = c.108).*

At sight *You're going to make a tune using this rhythm and at least three pitches. This is the pulse (two bars at ♩ = c.108). You now have half a minute to try it out. After half a minute: I'll now count you in for two bars (at ♩ = c.108).*

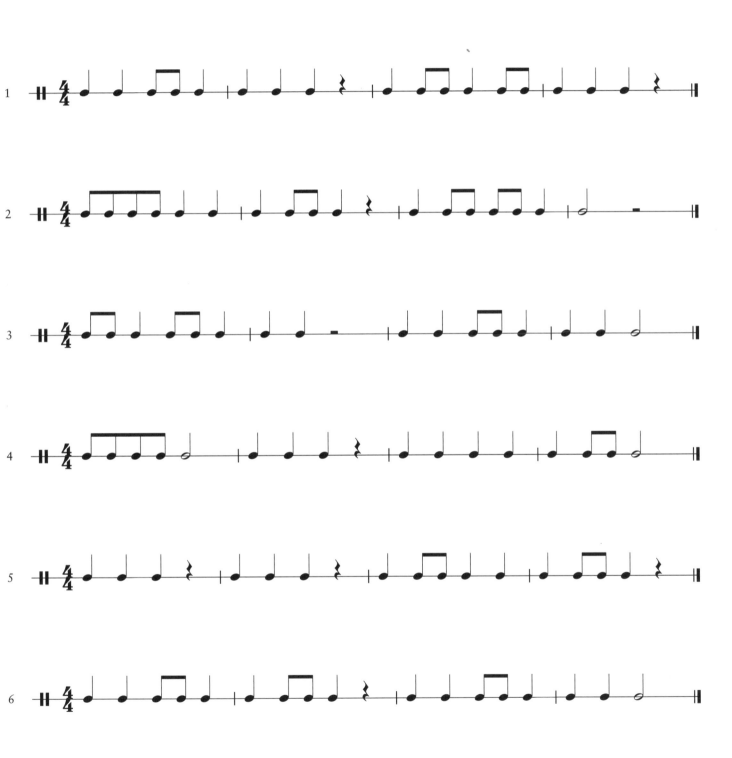

Question & Answer

Have a look at this test, where you're going to play the given part and make up an answer. You have half a minute to try it out and then I'll count you in. Here is the pulse (two bars at ♩ = c.108). After half a minute: I'll now count you in for two bars (at ♩ = c.108).

Sight-Reading

You have half a minute to look through this piece of music and, if you wish, try out any part or parts of it on your instrument.
I'll then ask you to play it.

silver

Call & Response

I'm going to play you a phrase and then I want you to answer me. I'll then continue with another phrase for you to answer.
We're in … (key) and my first note is … (pitch, named and played). I'll count myself in for two bars.

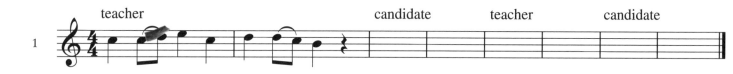

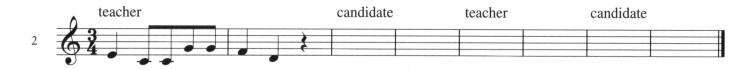

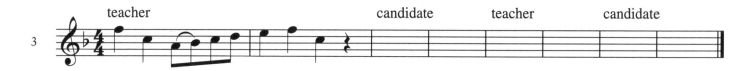

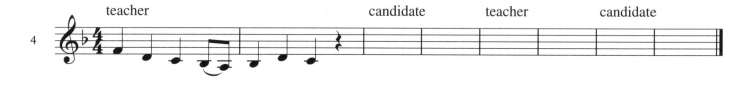

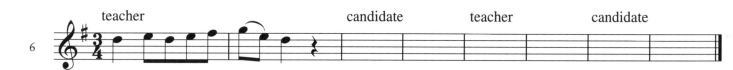

Make a Tune

You're going to make a tune in (C, F majors) *using this rhythm and at least five pitches. This is the pulse (two bars at ♩ = c.108).*
You now have half a minute to try it out. After half a minute: *I'll now count you in for two bars (at ♩ = c.108).*

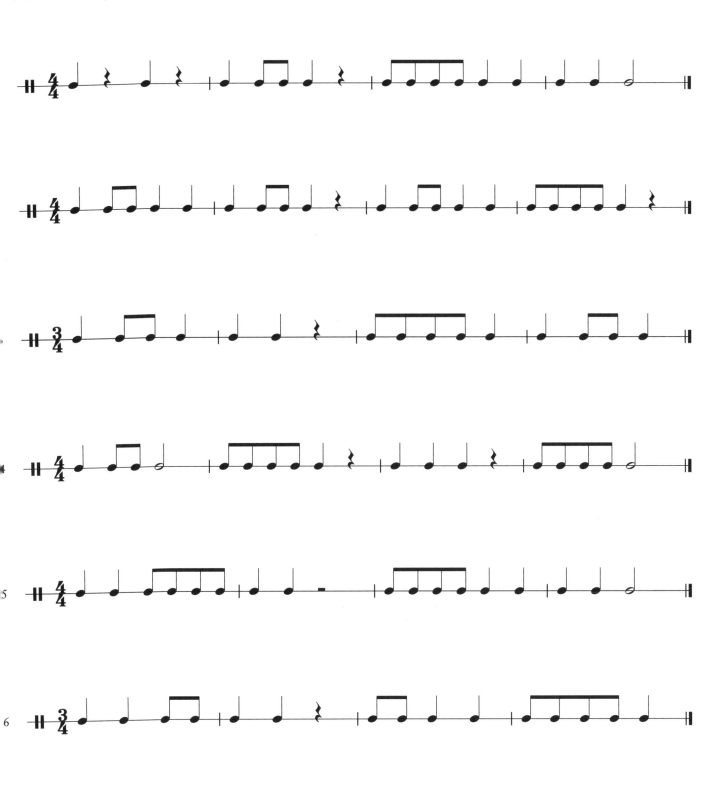

Question & Answer

Have a look at this test, where you're going to play the given part and make up an answer. You have half a minute to try it out and then I'll count you in. Here is the pulse (two bars at ♩ = c.108). After half a minute: I'll now count you in for two bars (at ♩ = c.108).

AB 3031

Sight-Reading

You have half a minute to look through this piece of music and, if you wish, try out any part or parts of it on your instrument. I'll then ask you to play it.

gold

Call & Response

I'm going to play you a phrase and then I want you to answer me. I'll then continue with another phrase for you to answer. We're in … (key) and my first note is … (pitch, named and played). I'll count myself in for two bars.

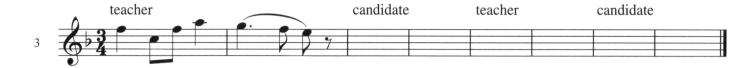

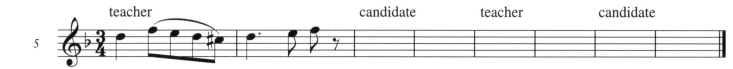

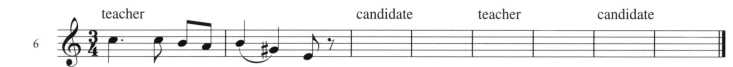

Make a Tune

You're going to make a tune in (C, F, G majors; A minor) *using this rhythm and at least five pitches. This is the pulse (two bars at ♩ = c.108). You now have half a minute to try it out. After half a minute: I'll now count you in for two bars (at ♩ = c.108).*

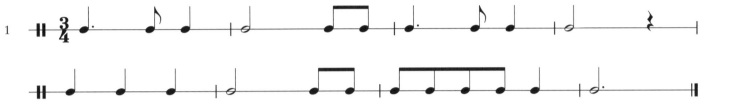

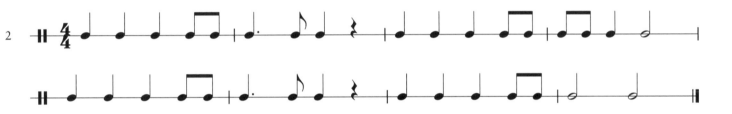

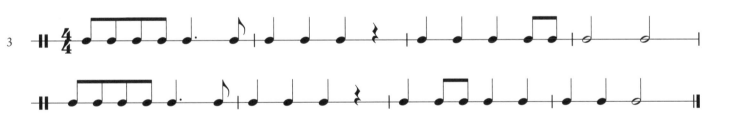

cont.

You're going to make a tune in (C, F, G majors; A minor) *using this rhythm and at least five pitches. This is the pulse (two bars at ♩ = c.108). You now have half a minute to try it out.* After half a minute: *I'll now count you in for two bars* (at ♩ = c.108).

4

5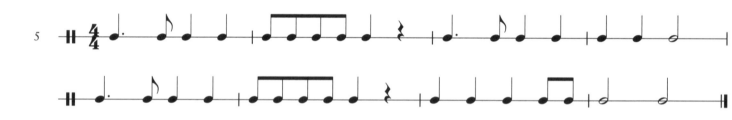

6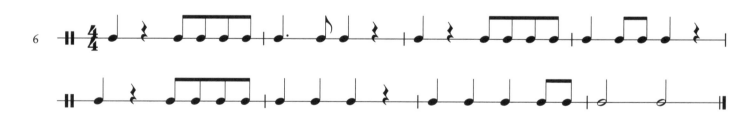

AB 3031

Question & Answer

Have a look at this test, where you're going to play the given part and make up an answer. You have half a minute to try it out and then I'll count you in. Here is the pulse (two bars at ♩ = c.108). After half a minute: I'll now count you in for two bars (at ♩ = c.108).

Sight-Reading

*You have half a minute to look through this piece of music and, if you wish, try out any part or parts of it on your instrument.
I'll then ask you to play it.*

platinum

Call & Response

I'm going to play you a phrase and then I want you to answer me. I'll then continue with another phrase for you to answer.
We're in … (key) and my first note is … (pitch, named and played). I'll count myself in for two bars.

Make a Tune

You're going to make a tune in (C, F, G, B♭ majors; A, D minors) using this rhythm and at least five pitches. This is the pulse (two bars at ♩ = c.108). You now have half a minute to try it out. After half a minute: I'll now count you in for two bars (at ♩ = c.108).

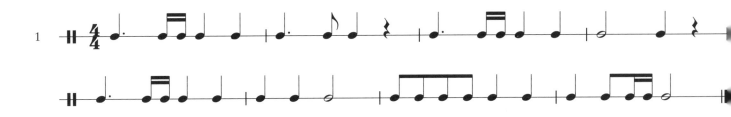

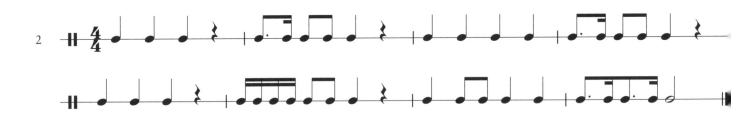

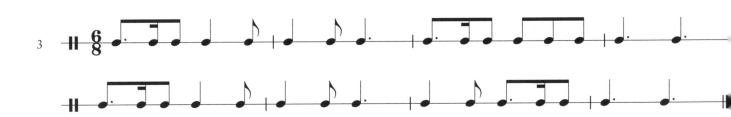

AB 3031

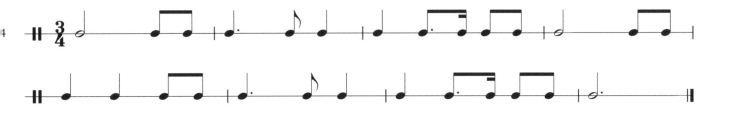

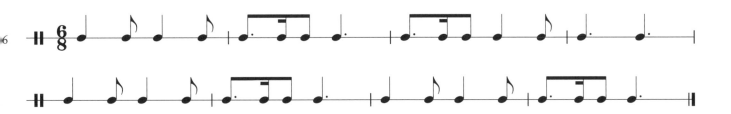

Question & Answer

Have a look at this test, where you're going to play the given part and make up an answer. You have half a minute to try it out and then I'll count you in. Here is the pulse (two bars at ♩ = c.108). After half a minute: I'll now count you in for two bars (at ♩ = c.108).

Sight-Reading

You have half a minute to look through this piece of music and, if you wish, try out any part or parts of it on your instrument.
I'll then ask you to play it.

SAMPLE DOWNLOAD PAGE

Copper Options
Teacher's Page

Royal Academy of Music
Royal College of Music
Royal Northern College of Music
Royal Scottish Academy of Music and Dr

ASSOCIATED BOAR
OF THE ROYAL SCHOOLS OF MUS

Call & Response

I'm going to play you a phrase and then I want you to answer me. I'll then continue with another phrase for you to answer.
We're in … (key) and my first note is … (pitch, named and played). I'll count myself in for two bars.

Make a Tune

By ear *You're going to make a tune using at least three pitches. Use the rhythm that I'm about to clap; you'll hear this three times.*
You'll then have half a minute to prepare. This is the pulse (two bars at ♩ = c.108/54). Here's the rhythm for the first/second/third time.
After half a minute: I'll now count you in for two bars (at ♩ = c.108/54).

At sight *You're going to make a tune using this rhythm and at least three pitches. This is the pulse (two bars at ♩ = c.108/54).*
You now have half a minute to try it out. After half a minute: I'll now count you in for two bars (at ♩ = c.108/54).

Set 1 *or*

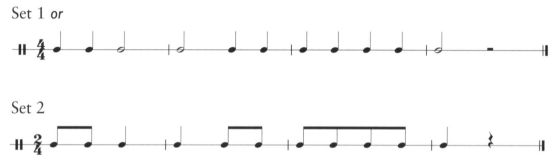

Set 2

Question & Answer

You will hear two rhythms in 4 time (at ♩ = c.108). After each rhythm, play it back in time and as an echo. You can use just one pitch, or
more if you wish. I'll count in two bars (at ♩ = c.108) before giving the first rhythm.

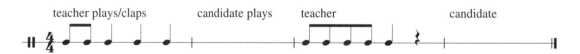

Sight-Reading

You have half a minute to look through this piece of music and, if you wish, try out any part or parts of it on your instrument.
I'll then ask you to play it.

To be returned with the video to Music Medals, The Associated Board, 24 Portland Place, London W1B 1LU

Bronze Options

Teacher's Page

Royal Academy of Music
Royal College of Music
Royal Northern College of Music
Royal Scottish Academy of Music and Drama

ASSOCIATED BOARD
OF THE ROYAL SCHOOLS OF MUSIC

Call & Response

I'm going to play you a phrase and then I want you to answer me. I'll then continue with another phrase for you to answer.
We're in … (key) and my first note is … (pitch, named and played). I'll count myself in for two bars.

Make a Tune

By ear *You're going to make a tune using at least three pitches. Use the rhythm that I'm about to clap; you'll hear this three times.*
You'll then have half a minute to prepare. This is the pulse (two bars at ♩ = c.108). Here's the rhythm for the first/second/third time.
After half a minute: I'll now count you in for two bars (at ♩ = c.108).

At sight *You're going to make a tune using this rhythm and at least three pitches. This is the pulse (two bars at ♩ = c.108).*
You now have half a minute to try it out. After half a minute: I'll now count you in for two bars (at ♩ = c.108).

Question & Answer

Have a look at this test, where you're going to play the given part and make up an answer. You have half a minute to try it out and then
I'll count you in. Here is the pulse (two bars at ♩ = c.108). After half a minute: I'll now count you in for two bars (at ♩ = c.108).

Sight-Reading

You have half a minute to look through this piece of music and, if you wish, try out any part or parts of it on your instrument.
I'll then ask you to play it.

To be returned with the video to Music Medals, The Associated Board, 24 Portland Place, London W1B 1LU

music medals

SAMPLE DOWNLOAD PAGE

Silver Options
Teacher's Page

Royal Academy of Music
Royal College of Music
Royal Northern College of Music
Royal Scottish Academy of Music and

ASSOCIATED BOAR
OF THE ROYAL SCHOOLS OF MUS

Call & Response

I'm going to play you a phrase and then I want you to answer me. I'll then continue with another phrase for you to answer.
We're in … (key) and my first note is … (pitch, named and played). I'll count myself in for two bars.

Make a Tune

You're going to make a tune in F major using this rhythm and at least five pitches. This is the pulse (two bars at ♩ = c.108).
You now have half a minute to try it out. After half a minute: I'll now count you in for two bars (at ♩ = c.108).

Question & Answer

Have a look at this test, where you're going to play the given part and make up an answer. You have half a minute to try it out and then
I'll count you in. Here is the pulse (two bars at ♩ = c.108). After half a minute: I'll now count you in for two bars (at ♩ = c.108).

Sight-Reading

You have half a minute to look through this piece of music and, if you wish, try out any part or parts of it on your instrument.
I'll then ask you to play it.

To be returned with the video to Music Medals, The Associated Board, 24 Portland Place, London W1B 1LU